THE OFFICIAL
ASTON VILLA

ANNUAL 2010

A Grange Publication

Compiled by Rob Bishop and Mark Clayton
Special thanks to Gayner Monkton and Lorna McClelland

Photographs © PA Photos, Neville Williams, Mark Clayton, Tricia Mills and Rob Bishop

ISBN 978-1-906-211-72-1

£6.99

CLUB HONOURS

European Cup
Winners: 1982
Quarter-finalists: 1982-83

European Super Cup
Winners: 1982-83

World Club Championship
1982

Inter Toto Cup
Winners: 2001

Football League
Champions: 1893-94, 1895-96, 1896-97,
1898-99, 1899-1900, 1909-10, 1980-81
Runners-up: 1888-89, 1902-03, 1907-08,
1910-11, 1912-13, 1913-14, 1930-31,
1932-33, 1989-90

Premiership
Runners-up: 1992-93

Division Two
Champions: 1937-38, 1959-60

Division Three
Champions: 1971-72

FA Cup
Winners: 1887, 1895, 1897,
1905, 1913, 1920, 1957
Runners-up: 1892, 1924, 2000

League Cup
Winners: 1961, 1975, 1977,
1994, 1996
Runners-up: 1963, 1971

FA Youth Cup
Winners: 1972, 1980, 2002
Runners-up: 1978, 2004

CONTENTS

BRAD FRIEDEL

HOLA CARLOS!

Footballers will often tell you they like "to do their talking on the pitch." Carlos Cuellar didn't have much option when he joined Villa – because he hardly spoke any English.

Despite having spent a year with Scottish giants Glasgow Rangers, the Spanish central defender's grasp of our language was still fairly limited when he arrived at Villa Park in August 2008. Initially, in fact, the only person he could really understand was young Glaswegian midfielder Barry Bannan!

But Carlos was determined that would have to change. Every day after training he watched two films with subtitles so he could check out words as they were being spoken, and his improvement was amazing.

"I really wanted to learn English," he says. "For me, watching films was the best way to do it."

Even before he was able to converse properly with his team-mates, though, Carlos was delighted with the welcome he received as a new Villa player.

"It was a big opportunity for me to come to one of the biggest clubs in the Premier League," he says. "From my first day, everyone was very friendly, which was a big help.

"Every day here is a dream for me because ever since I was young, I've wanted to play in England. I used to watch Manchester United and Liverpool a lot because they were always on television in Spain."

Having grown up in the Spanish capital, it's not surprising that Carlos is a big Real Madrid supporter, so he had to endure a lot of teasing from his Villa colleagues when Barcelona won the Champions League!

Regardless of his devotion to Real, however, he much prefers playing in this country to the days when he was with Spanish clubs Numancia and Osasuna.

"This is what I've always wanted," he says. "The football here is more honest. In Spain, you get a lot of diving and the game keeps being stopped.

"In England, players go in strongly for the ball but games are faster and more exciting."

ON THE BALL – CARLOS SIGNS
VILLA FOOTBALLS FOR CHARITY AT THE CLUB'S
BODYMOOR HEATH TRAINING GROUND

SPOT ON IN SPAIN!

We would all love to see Villa win a major trophy – and the club collected one piece of silverware even before the current season officially got under way.

Martin O'Neill's men lifted the Peace Cup in Spain, beating Italian giants Juventus on penalties in the final of the prestigious pre-season tournament. And just to underline what a fine achievement it was, the Italians had knocked out Real Madrid in the semi-finals.

It was certainly a night to remember in Seville. Villa and Juve were deadlocked at 0-0 after extra-time, and then it was down to the tension-charged business of spot kicks.

Youngsters Barry Bannan and Shane Lowry led the way for Villa, staying ice-cool as they both beat Gianluigi Buffon, one of the world's greatest goalkeepers.

And although Steve Sidwell had fired over from the second penalty, Villa led the shoot-out 3-2 when Ashley Young converted the team's fourth kick.

The pendulum swung back towards Juve when Felipe Melo brought the scores level before Chris Herd's effort was saved by Buffon.

That left Alessandro Del Piero with the opportunity to clinch victory for the Italians but the veteran marksman scuffed his shot, allowing goalkeeper Brad Guzan to make his second save of the shoot-out.

Then Carlos Cuellar planted his kick firmly in the corner – and when Juve missed their next kick, Villa were able to celebrate a memorable triumph.

Yet they must have been wondering after their opening match if they should book an early flight home.

They lost striker Emile Heskey with a head wound in the opening minutes against Malaga and never really got into their stride, eventually losing 1-0 to an 80th minute goal from Fernando.

That meant the team's fate was out of their own hands. If Malaga had avoided defeat by Atlante two nights later, Villa would have been out – but the Mexicans won 3-1 to throw out a claret-and-blue lifeline.

That meant all three teams in the group still had a chance of qualifying for the semi-finals, although Villa's prospects again looked bleak when they lost Stiliyan Petrov with a shoulder injury early in their match against Atlante and then went a goal down as Curtis Davies deflected the ball into his own net.

With Villa needing to win by two clear goals to qualify, their chances looked slim, but young winger Marc Albrighton fired home the equaliser, John Carew put them ahead, and Ashley Young headed the goal which secured a 3-1 victory and progress to the next stage.

The semi-final opponents were Portuguese club Porto, who beat Celtic in the UEFA Cup final when Martin O'Neill was in charge at Parkhead.

It was billed as a revenge mission for the Villa boss – and he made sure it was completed successfully.

Villa went two-up through Heskey and Steve Sidwell, and although the England striker was sent off for retaliation in the second half, Porto were restricted to a last-minute penalty from Hulk.

Then came the penalty drama which ended with Villa holding the cup aloft. Here's to more glory before the end of the season...

AUGUST

It's very much a new-look Villa squad who prepare for the 2008-09 season. Curtis Davies has officially become a Villan following his 12-month loan from West Bromwich Albion, while manager Martin O'Neill also splashes out on midfielders Steve Sidwell and James Milner, defenders Luke Young, Nicky Shorey and Carlos Cuellar, and American goalkeepers Brad Friedel and Brad Guzan.

The Premier League season gets off to a flying start. After a goalless first half against Manchester City at Villa Park, John Carew scores Villa's first domestic goal of the season two minutes after the interval.

And although City draw level, Gabby Agbonlahor then takes centre stage with a hat-trick in the space of eight minutes as Villa go on to win 4-2. Gabby's treble makes him the first Villa player for 78 years to score three times in the first league match of the season.

But pride often comes before a fall and that's the case for Villa. Six days later, they visit Stoke City optimistic of another

victory, only to suffer a 3-2 defeat at the hands of the Premier League new boys.

Villa twice draw level at the Britannia Stadium, thanks to Carew and skipper Martin Laursen, and it looks like they will at least head home with a point. But in the fourth minute of stoppage time, one of Rory Delap's infamous long throws is headed past Friedel by substitute Mamady Sidibe to give the Potters an unlikely 3-2 victory.

It's a major disappointment for Martin O'Neill's men but they recover to take a point from a goalless draw at home to Liverpool on the last day of the month.

"EVERY PLAYER WANTS TO SCORE GOALS AND IT WAS GREAT TO HAVE A START LIKE THAT. I GOT THE MATCH BALL SIGNED BY ALL OUR PLAYERS." **GABBY AGBONLAHOR**

PREMIER LEAGUE POSITION: 3RD

It's a maximum month for Villa as far as the Premier League is concerned. Martin O'Neill's men go roaring up to third in the table with three consecutive 2-1 victories – two of them on opposition territory.

More than eight years had elapsed since the club's last victory at White Hart Lane but it's clear from the opening minutes that an unproductive run is about to be broken.

After just five minutes, Nigel Reo-Coker claims his first Villa league goal, sidefooting home at the far post after John Carew has cleverly flicked on Gabby Agbonlahor's low left-wing centre.

When Ashley Young fires home the second on 54 minutes, the visitors are cruising, and Darren Bent's late effort for Spurs is no more than a minor inconvenience.

Villa aren't quite as dominant at The Hawthorns as they had been in north London, but two goals in three minutes are enough to secure victory over West Bromwich Albion.

Carew heads the first before Agbonlahor fires a low angled drive past former Villa on-loan goalkeeper and into the far corner. Once again, the opposition goal, this time from James Morrison, is merely a consolation.

It's a slightly different story when Sunderland came to Villa Park. This time, our opponents take the lead, Djibril Cisse drilling home a low shot after just 10 minutes.

But Ashley Young's superb dipping free-kick brings the scores level before Carew clinches all three points with a cheeky back-heel through his own legs from close range.

Victory over the Black Cats is the perfect reaction to a 1-0 Carling Cup defeat at home to Queens Park Rangers three days earlier.

"IT'S GOOD TO GET A GOAL OCCASIONALLY BUT THIS GAME IS ALL ABOUT WINNING. THAT'S ALL I WANT TO DO." NIGEL REO-COKER

OCTOBER

"MY GOAL AT WIGAN IS UP THERE WITH MY BEST. IT WAS NICE TO BE INVOLVED AND TO SCORE WAS THE ICING ON THE CAKE." **STEVE SIDWELL**

PREMIER LEAGUE POSITION: 4TH

Despite a 2-0 defeat at Chelsea and a goalless home draw against Portsmouth, Villa are back to winning ways with a vengeance, scoring seven goals in two matches in the space of four days.

A 4-0 victory over Wigan Athletic at the JJB Stadium is arguably a little flattering to Martin O'Neill's men. Gareth Barry opens the scoring from the penalty spot after Gabby Agbonlahor is brought down, but only a couple of fine saves from Brad Friedel keep Villa ahead at the interval.

The home side also create a few second half chances, too, although the result is rarely in doubt after Agbonlahor scores Villa's second in the 57th minute.

Five minutes later, substitute John Carew heads home a cross from Gabby to make it 3-0 – and another substitute completes the scoring right at the end.

There are only five minutes remaining when Steve Sidwell replaces Stiliyan Petrov, but the former Reading and Chelsea midfielder marks his league debut for Villa

with a thundering drive into the top corner of the net.

A few days after Sidwell's first goal in claret and blue, there's another one to celebrate. This time it's full-back Luke Young, who is on target and while it's an untidy nudge from a couple of yards, it's more than welcome as Villa drew level against Blackburn on the stroke of half-time.

Barry converts James Milner's low cross to put Villa ahead in the 64th minute, with Agbonlahor adding number three before Brett Emerton's stoppage time goal brings the final score to 3-2.

It's a strange month for Villa as the team's form dips alarmingly and then soars to great heights within the space of a few weeks.

A 2-0 defeat by Newcastle United at St James' Park is followed by an even bigger disappointment as Steve Sidwell's late error presents Turkish striker Tuncay with a late winner for Middlesbrough at Villa Park after the midfielder had earlier produced Villa's equaliser.

With two consecutive defeats behind them, the team's prospects look bleak indeed as they travel to the Emirates Stadium six days after the 2-1 home reversal at the hands of Boro.

But nothing in football is ever predictable, and just when Martin O'Neill's men look ripe for slaughter, they produce a stunning 2-0 victory over high-riding Arsenal.

The result is no fluke either, with Villa producing some outstanding football to outsmart and then out-gun the Gunners.

With the visitors well on top from the start, several first half chances go begging, including an Ashley Young penalty which is saved by goalkeeper Manuel Almunia.

But Villa's poise and patience is finally rewarded when Arsenal defender Gael Clichy, under pressure from Gabby Agbonlahor, heads Young's 70th minute cross into his own net.

And 10 minutes later, Gabby moves on to a long clearance from skipper Martin Laursen to outpace William Gallas and fire a low shot inside the near post from the edge of the penalty area.

A week later, MON's men once again prove they can mix it with the best, sharing a goalless draw with Manchester United at Villa Park.

And while another 0-0 at home to Fulham seven days later is something of a disappointment, three consecutive league games without defeat sets a healthy trend for the boys in claret and blue.

Villa's impressive form earns an England debut for Agbonlahor against Germany in Berlin, the young striker producing an excellent performance in a 2-1 win before being replaced by Villa team-mate Ashley Young in the 77th minute.

"WE PLAYED BRILLIANTLY FROM START TO FINISH AT ARSENAL AND THERE WAS A TREMENDOUS ENERGY AND VITALITY ABOUT THE TEAM." **MARTIN O'NEILL**

DECEMBER

A small piece of club history is made as Steve Sidwell scores in the first minute and Ashley Young in the last in a 3-2 victory over Everton at Goodison Park.

It's the first time Villa have scored in the opening minute and then grabbed a winning goal in the final minute. Sidwell's goal, a stunning right-foot shot after just 34 seconds, is also the fastest in the Barclays Premier League so far this season, although it gives no indication of the drama to follow.

Everton draw through Joleon Lescott, with Young restoring Villa's lead when he moves on to a back pass from Phil Jagielka to fire past goalkeeper Tim Howard.

But then it's very much backs-to-the-wall as the Merseysiders surge forward in search of a second equaliser, which finally arrives when Lescott volleys home his second goal in the third minute of stoppage time.

Surely there's no time for anything more? Amazingly, there is. Almost immediately, Gabby Agbonlahor slips a short pass to Young, who accelerates past Lescott before calmly firing past the advancing Howard and into the bottom corner. Phew – what a finish!

"WHEN ARSENAL WENT TWO UP WE THOUGHT IT WASN'T GOING TO BE OUR DAY. TO EQUALISE SO LATE ALMOST FELT LIKE WE HAD WON."
ZAT KNIGHT

The following week, Villa are again in the mood for goals, beating Bolton Wanderers 4-2. Agbonlahor is on target twice against the Trotters, while Young adds another to his tally and Villa's other goal comes via Bolton striker Kevin Davies, who heads into his own net under pressure from Martin Laursen

There's another own goal as Villa make it three wins on the trot just before Christmas, Young's shot deflecting in off Hammers' full-back Lucas Neill to give Martin O'Neill's men a 1-0 verdict – and yet another at Hull City at the end of the month.

On this occasion, Young's cross is prodded in by Kamil Zayatte to give Villa another 1-0 success – and in between times there's a thrilling 2-2 draw against Arsenal at Villa Park.

Despite being well on top, Villa go two-down against the Gunners by the 48th minute, but Gareth Barry reduces the deficit from the penalty spot and Zat Knight pops up with an equaliser in stoppage time.

Villa's unbeaten run earns Martin O'Neill the Barclays manager of the month award, while Ashley Young is voted player of the month.

PREMIER LEAGUE POSITION: 4TH

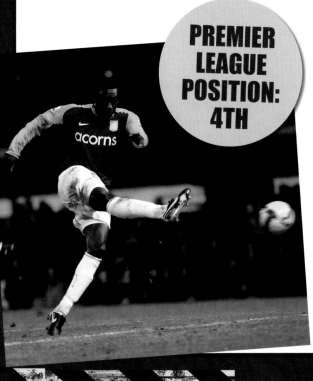

"IT WAS A GREAT START FOR ME. I'D NEVER SCORED ON A DEBUT BEFORE." **EMILE HESKEY**

PREMIER LEAGUE POSITION: 4TH

Happy birthday James Milner! Villa launch the new year with a 2-1 third round FA Cup win over Gillingham at the Priestfield Stadium, where Milner scores twice – including the winner from a 78th minute penalty in the absence of Gareth Barry. It's Milner's first spot kick for Villa, although he's scored a few for England under-21s.

The team's first Cup win for nearly three years is followed by two more 2-1 victories as Martin O'Neill's men maintain their momentum in the league.

First, neighbours West Bromwich Albion are beaten at Villa Park, where defender Curtis Davies opens the scoring with a brave diving header before former Villa goalkeeper Scott Carson diverts Gabby Agbonlahor's hard low cross into his own net. It's initially awarded as an own goal but the Dubious Goals Panel subsequently rule it should be credited to Gabby.

Then, at the Stadium of Light a week later, Villa overcome Sunderland by the same margin after Danny Collins gives the home side an early lead.

Although the visitors are not at their best, they are thrown a lifeline when Milner lunges to convert Ashley Young's low cross in the six-yard box. And with 10 minutes remaining, even though Villa are down to 10 men after Young is sent off for a foul on home skipper Dean Whitehead, Gareth Barry drives home a penalty to ensure all three points.

Villa have to settle for a goalless draw in their fourth round FA Cup-tie against Championship club Doncaster Rovers at the Keepmoat Stadium but the following Tuesday they are back to winning ways with three more Premier League points.

England striker Emile Heskey, signed from Wigan Athletic the previous week, marks his debut with a super strike to clinch a 1-0 verdict at Fratton Park.

Heskey, though, is unable to repeat his scoring act against his former club Wigan a few days later, the Latics sneaking away from Villa Park with a 0-0 draw. The good news is that John Carew, sidelined by injury for more than two months, is back in action.

FEBRUARY

"I DON'T THINK WE WERE THAT BAD AGAINST CHELSEA. ON ANOTHER DAY WE WOULD HAVE SCORED TWO OR THREE." **ASHLEY YOUNG**

A 3-1 replay victory over Doncaster Rovers takes Villa through to the fifth round of the FA Cup. Steve Sidwell and John Carew are on target in the opening 19 minutes and although Jason Price reduces the deficit just before half-time, a glancing header from teenager Nathan Delfouneso secures Villa's passage.

But that's nothing compared with the celebrations at Ewood Park three days later as Villa beat Blackburn Rovers 2-0 to create a club record seven consecutive away wins in league matches.

James Milner opens the scoring with a stunning angled drive through a crowded goalmouth, with Gabby Agbonlahor making absolutely sure of the points when he latches on to a poor clearance to fire home number two in the final minute.

Later that evening, Villa create another club record when six of their players – Milner, Agbonlahor, Gareth Barry, Emile Heskey, Ashley Young and Luke Young are named in Fabio Capello's England squad.

Only Barry and Heskey are actually involved in the friendly against Spain in Seville but never before have six Villa players been called up by England.

Unfortunately, Villa's FA Cup run comes to an end with a fifth round defeat by Everton at Goodison Park the following weekend, despite a ninth-minute penalty

equaliser
from Milner – and then
another run is ended.

After going 13 league games without defeat in the Premier League – only two short of an all-time record – MON's men go down 1-0 at home to Chelsea and surrender third place in the table to the Londoners. It's a tightly-fought game but Frank Lampard's first half goal proves decisive.

Villa haven't done very well in March since the start of the new millennium – and unfortunately 2009 is no different. For the third year running, the team fail to record a single victory during this particular month.

But how close they come against struggling Stoke City. Bulgarian star Stiliyan Petrov opens the scoring with his first home goal since arriving from Celtic two-and-a-half years earlier – a powerful shot from the edge of the penalty area.

And substitute John Carew's 79th minute effort is even more spectacular. Petrov's cross is driven a touch too hard but the Norwegian striker sticks out his right foot for a sensational volley which flies just under the bar from 20 yards.

Two-up with 11 minutes to go, Villa appear to have the game won. But you can never take anything for granted in football. With three minutes remaining, Ryan Shawcross heads what appears to be a consolation goal – and Glenn Whelan's stoppage time shot earns the visitors a 2-2 draw.

In the event, that turns out to be Villa's only point of the month. A 2-0 defeat by Manchester City at Eastlands a few days later is followed by a surprise 2-1 home defeat by Tottenham Hotspur, Carew's 85th minute header coming too late to spark a revival.

Worse still, Villa slump to a 5-0 defeat at the hands of rampant Liverpool at Anfield.

To make matters worse, goalkeeper Brad Friedel is sent off for bringing down Fernando Torres, although the American's red card is later rescinded.

PREMIER LEAGUE POSITION: 5TH

"MY GOAL AGAINST STOKE IS DEFINITELY IN MY TOP FIVE. I'M NOT GOING TO SAY IT'S MY BEST EVER BECAUSE I'VE SCORED A LOT OF OTHER GOALS WHICH HAVE BEEN PLEASING. BUT I WOULD RANK IT AMONG MY BEST." **JOHN CAREW**

APRIL

Football can be a cruel game, as Villa discover against Manchester United at Old Trafford. Despite falling behind to a Cristiano Ronaldo goal, Martin O'Neill's men battle back for an equaliser when John Carew heads home a Gareth Barry cross at United's famous Stretford End.

And when Gabby Agbonlahor bravely lunges in front of goalkeeper Edwin Van Der Sar to put the visitors ahead in the 58th minute, we even start dreaming of the club's first away win over the Reds since 1983.

Unfortunately, United have other ideas. After Ronaldo brings the scores level again with a shot from outside the penalty area, Italian teenager Federico Macheda breaks Villa hearts with an amazing stoppage time winner on his debut.

If that comeback is one to forget from a claret and blue perspective, there's one to savour the following week. Twice trailing by two goals at home to Everton, Villa refuse to submit, eventually forcing a 3-3 draw thanks to a John Carew goal, a superb James Milner free-kick and a Gareth Barry penalty.

Six days later, there's another stalemate, this time against West Ham United. Emile Heskey scores his first home goal following a flowing move, to establish an interval lead, only for the visitors to sneak away with a 1-1 draw thanks to Diego Tristan's late equaliser.

This match is significant for more than just the result. Villa have to play in their all-white third kit because the Hammers' all-blue shirt clashes with the sleeves of our regular claret and blue outfit.

It's all-square, too, against Bolton Wanderers at the Reebok Stadium, Villa's goal coming from Ashley Young, who is named PFA Young Footballer of the Year the following day.

And to underline what a fine crop of young talent the club have at their disposal, Gabby Agbonlahor finishes runner-up in the voting.

"IT WAS NICE TO GET MY FIRST GOAL AT VILLA PARK – BUT DISAPPOINTING NOT TO GET A SECOND WHEN I HIT A POST."
EMILE HESKEY

PREMIER LEAGUE POSITION: 5TH

A victory at last – and what a relief! Since their record-breaking seventh consecutive league away win at Blackburn in February, Villa have failed to win in 12 league and cup matches, so a 1-0 verdict at home to Hull City is more than welcome.

John Carew is the man who grabs the only goal of the game, providing a deft close-range finish past former Villa goalkeeper Boaz Myhill following a Gareth Barry pass and a fine centre from Ashley Young.

Unfortunately, Martin O'Neill's men slip up the following Saturday, losing 3-1 to Fulham at Craven Cottage despite a well-taken equaliser by Young, who slots the ball home at the far post from James Milner's low right-wing cross.

That leaves just two games to go – both of them against teams battling for Premier League survival.

At The Riverside on the penultimate weekend of the season, Villa struggle in the first half, falling behind to an overhead kick from Middlesbrough's Turkish striker Tuncay.

But it's a completely different story after the interval as the visitors take control and create a succession of chances. As it is, they take only one, Carew turning sharply to fire home through a crowded goalmouth to earn a 1-1 draw.

The result effectively condemns a Boro side managed by former Villa skipper Gareth Southgate to relegation – and a week later the boys in claret and blue send another North East club into the Championship.

A first half own goal by Damien Duff, who diverts Gareth Barry's fierce shot past goalkeeper Steve Harper, ensures a 1-0 victory over Alan Shearer's side and means Villa end a long, long season on a high note.

Everton's 2-0 win at Fulham on the same afternoon means the team just miss out on fifth place but they finish with 62 points – two more than the previous season.

PREMIER LEAGUE POSITION: 6TH

"IT WASN'T ABOUT NEWCASTLE TRYING TO STAY UP, DOING FAVOURS FOR THEM OR DOING FAVOURS FOR ANYONE ELSE. IT WAS ABOUT WINNING." **CURTIS DAVIES**

UEFA CUP FOCUS
Back on the Euro trail

It all came to an end on a bitterly cold night in Moscow, but European football was well and truly back on the Villa agenda last season.

Six years after the clubs' previous UEFA Cup venture, Martin O'Neill and his players embarked on an adventure which took them to Denmark, Iceland, Bulgaria, the Czech Republic, Germany and Russia – with Villa Park visits from teams in Holland and Slovakia thrown in for good measure. It was certainly a time for brushing up on your geography!

A sixth place finish in the Premier League the previous season wasn't enough to secure automatic UEFA qualification, so Villa had to start their Euro trail in the Intertoto Cup.

Danish club Odense were the opponents at a time when many people were still on the beach, and after a 2-2 away draw in the first leg, thanks to goals from John Carew and Martin Laursen, an Ashley Young goal secured a 1-0 win at Villa Park.

That ensured progress to the UEFA Cup second qualifying round, where Villa were drawn against Icelandic opposition for the first time since beating Valur on the way to European Cup glory in 1981-82.

The tie against FH Hafnarfjordur was effectively over after the first leg in Reykjavik, where goals from Gareth Barry, Ashley Young, Gabby Agbonlahor and Laursen secured a comfortable 4-1 result. The return leg finished 1-1 after Craig Gardner had opened the scoring.

Villa were now in the competition proper, and there was a similar story in the first round against Litex

Lovech. Despite going behind in Bulgaria, Villa won 3-1 thanks to Nigel Reo-Coker, Stiliyan Petrov and a Gareth Barry penalty.

Back at Villa Park, though, it was another struggle, although Marlon Harewood scored a superb goal in a 1-1 draw.

Next up were the group stages and the opening match at home to Ajax was a truly memorable European night. Villa Park erupted when Laursen headed an early goal and although the Dutch masters equalised, Barry hit the winner just before half-time.

Moscow, Villa needed a second half equaliser from Carew to earn a 1-1 home draw in the first leg, having fallen behind to a goal from free-scoring Brazilian Vagner Love.

That meant the second leg in the Russian capital was always going to be extremely difficult, and so it proved. A Villa side including youngsters Barry Bannan and Marc Albrighton battled bravely but CSKA were too strong for them on the night, running out 2-0 winners.

In the round of 16, CSKA were beaten by Ukrainians Shakhtar Donetsk – who went on to win the trophy by beating German club Werder Bremen 2-1 in the final. The game in Istanbul marked the end of an era – from the start of this season the competition was renamed the Europa League.

John Carew deflected a Steve Sidwell shot into the far corner to clinch a 1-0 success away to Slavia Prague in the second game and Villa were virtually through to the knockout stages.

Unfortunately they lost the other two games in Group F, going down 2-1 at home to Slovakians MSK Zilina and 3-1 away to Bundesliga giants Hamburg SV, but those results were of no real significance as MON's men qualified for the knockout stages.

Unfortunately, their run came to an end in the round of 32. Drawn against Russian giants CSKA

Date	Opponents	Result	Scorers
Aug 17	MANCHESTER CITY	4-2	Agbonlahor 3, Carew
Aug 23	STOKE CITY	2-3	Carew, Laursen
Aug 31	LIVERPOOL	0-0	
Sep 15	TOTTENHAM HOTSPUR	2-1	Reo-Coker, A Young
Sep 21	WEST BROMWICH ALBION	2-1	Carew, Agbonlahor
Sep 27	SUNDERLAND	2-1	A Young , Carew
Oct 5	CHELSEA	0-2	
Oct 18	PORTSMOUTH	0-0	
Oct 26	WIGAN ATHLETIC	4-0	Barry pen, Agbonlahor, Carew, Sidwell
Oct 29	BLACKBURN ROVERS	3-2	L Young, Barry, Agbonlahor
Nov 3	NEWCASTLE UNITED	0-2	
Nov 9	MIDDLESBROUGH	1-2	Sidwell
Nov 15	ARSENAL	2-0	Clichy og, Agbonlahor
Nov 22	MANCHESTER UNITED	0-0	
Nov 29	FULHAM	0-0	
Dec 7	EVERTON	3-2	Sidwell, A Young 2
Dec 13	BOLTON WANDERERS	4-2	Agbonlahor 2, A Young, Davies og
Dec 20	WEST HAM UNITED	1-0	Neill og
Dec 26	ARSENAL	2-2	Barry pen, Knight
Dec 30	HULL CITY	1-0	Zayatte og
Jan 10	WEST BROMWICH ALBION	2-1	Davies, Agbonlahor
Jan 17	SUNDERLAND	2-1	Barry pen, Milner
Jan 27	PORTSMOUTH	1-0	Heskey
Jan 31	WIGAN ATHLETIC	0-0	
Feb 7	BLACKBURN ROVERS	2-0	Milner, Agbonlahor
Feb 21	CHELSEA	0-1	
Mar 1	STOKE CITY	2-2	Petrov, Carew
Mar 4	MANCHESTER CITY	0-2	
Mar 15	TOTTENHAM HOTSPUR	1-2	Carew
Mar 22	LIVERPOOL	0-5	
Apl 5	MANCHESTER UNITED	2-3	Carew, Agbonlahor
Apl 12	EVERTON	3-3	Carew, Milner, Barry pen
Apl 18	WEST HAM UNITED	1-1	Heskey
Apl 25	BOLTON WANDERERS	1-1	A Young
May 2	HULL CITY	1-0	Carew
May 9	FULHAM	1-3	A Young
May 16	MIDDLESBROUGH	1-1	Carew
May 24	NEWCASTLE UNITED	1-0	Duff og

JAMES MILNER

	Home						Away					
	P	W	D	L	F	A	W	D	L	F	A	Pts
1 Manchester United	38	16	2	1	43	13	12	4	3	25	11	90
2 Liverpool	38	12	7	0	41	13	13	4	2	36	14	86
3 Chelsea	38	11	6	2	33	12	14	2	3	35	12	83
4 Arsenal	38	11	5	3	31	16	9	7	3	37	21	72
5 Everton	38	8	6	5	31	20	9	6	4	24	17	63
6 ASTON VILLA	38	7	9	3	27	21	10	2	7	27	27	62
7 Fulham	38	11	3	5	28	16	3	8	8	11	18	53
8 Tottenham Hotspur	38	10	5	4	21	10	4	4	11	24	35	51
9 West Ham United	38	9	2	8	23	22	5	7	7	19	23	51
10 Manchester City	38	13	0	6	40	18	2	5	12	18	32	50
11 Wigan Athletic	38	8	5	6	17	18	4	4	11	17	27	45
12 Stoke City	38	10	5	4	22	15	2	4	13	16	40	45
13 Bolton Wanderers	38	7	5	7	21	21	4	3	12	20	32	41
14 Portsmouth	38	8	3	8	26	29	2	8	9	12	28	41
15 Blackburn Rovers	38	6	7	6	22	23	4	4	11	18	37	41
16 Sunderland	38	6	3	10	21	25	3	6	10	13	29	36
17 Hull City	38	3	8	11	18	36	5	6	8	21	28	35
18 Newcastle United	38	5	7	7	24	29	2	6	11	16	30	34
19 Middlesbrough	38	5	9	5	17	20	2	2	15	11	37	32
20 West Bromwich Albion	38	7	3	9	26	33	1	5	13	10	34	32

RESULTS AT A GLANCE CUP-TIES

INTERTOTO CUP

July 19	Odense	2-2	Carew, Laursen
July 26	Odense	1-0	A Young

UEFA CUP

Aug 14	Hafnarfjordur	4-1	Barry, A Young, Agbonlahor, Laursen
Aug 28	Hafnarfjordur	1-1	Gardner
Sep 18	Litex Lovech	3-1	Reo-Coker, Barry, Petrov
Oct 2	Litex Lovech	1-1	Harewood
Oct 23	Ajax	2-1	Laursen, Barry
Nov 6	Slavia Prague	1-0	Carew
Dec 4	MSK Zilina	1-2	Delfouneso
Dec 17	Hamburg SV	1-3	Delfouneso
Feb 18	CSKA Moscow	1-1	Carew
Feb 26	CSKA Moscow	0-2	

FA CUP

Jan 4	Gillingham	2-1	Milner 2 (1 pen)
Jan 24	Doncaster Rovers	0-0	
Feb 4	Doncaster Rovers	3-1	Sidwell, Carew, Delfouneso
Feb 15	Everton	1-3	Milner pen

LEAGUE CUP

Sep 24	QPR	0-1	

CURTIS DAVIES

Cool Carew

♪ John Carew, Carew, he's bigger than me and you, he's gonna score one or two... **or 15!** ♪

For the second consecutive season, the towering Norwegian striker was Villa's leading scorer – and his total would have been much higher had he not been sidelined by injury for more than two months.

As it was he still hit the target on 15 occasions – two more than the 13-goal haul which had put him top of the Villa scoring charts the previous season.

His spectacular volley against Stoke City was voted Villa's Goal of the Season, while he also netted the team's cheekiest and luckiest goals of the campaign.

In the eyes of Villa supporters, though, every one of them was special. Let's take a look at them...

1 ODENSE (a) 2-2

It's mid-July and a lot of people are still on the beach but John gets straight down to the business he knows best – scoring goals. Just seven minutes into the Intertoto Cup first leg in Denmark, he sends an unstoppable close-range drive into the roof of the net after Ashley Young's low shot is parried by the goalkeeper.

2 MANCHESTER CITY (h) 4-2

Gabby Agbonlahor is the hero of the opening Premier League match, netting a quickfire second half hat-trick – but not before Big John breaks the deadlock by heading home Ashley Young's 47th minute free-kick following good work by Gareth Barry.

3 STOKE CITY (a) 2-3

There's a disappointing outcome to the game at the Britannia Stadium but John's 63rd minute strike is a textbook goal. Playing the ball to Ashley Young, he takes the winger's back-heel return pass in his stride before hitting a right-foot angled drive past former Villa goalkeeper Thomas Sorensen and into the far corner.

4 WEST BROMWICH ALBION (a) 2-1

It's the Young-Carew combination yet again as Villa unlock the Baggies defence at The Hawthorns. This time the winger delivers a perfect free-kick, and John climbs to send a well-placed header in off the right-hand post.

5 SUNDERLAND (h) 2-1

This is surely Villa's cheekiest goal of the season. After Young's free-kick cannons off a defender, Stiliyan Petrov drives the ball hard and low across the goalmouth – and John converts from a few yards by side-footing the ball between his own legs!

6 WIGAN ATHLETIC (a) 4-0

John is on the bench at the JJB Stadium but once he gets on the pitch it doesn't take him long to put his name on the score sheet. Just 12 minutes after replacing Gareth Barry, the Norwegian heads home Gabby Agbonlahor's left-wing cross from a couple of yards.

7 SLAVIA PRAGUE (a) 1-0

If his goal against Sunderland was cheeky, John almost has a cheek claiming this one! Steve Sidwell deserves most of the credit for a powerful shot which hits John on his legs and diverts into the far corner of the net for Villa's winner in a UEFA Cup group game.

8 DONCASTER ROVERS (h) 3-1

Having missed the original tie at the Keepmoat Stadium because of his long lay-off, it doesn't take John long to make his mark in his first full game for nearly three months. His powerful 19th minute shot from just outside the penalty area takes a slight deflection past veteran goalkeeper Neil Sullivan to out Villa two-up.

9 CSKA MOSCOW (h) 1-1

This goal ultimately counts for nothing as Villa lose the second leg in Moscow but it's a fine effort which salvages a draw against the Russians at Villa Park. Although Ashley Young's centre flashes across the face of goal, Craig Gardner retrieves it beyond the far post and cuts it back for Carew to score with a powerful low 12-yard shot.

10 STOKE CITY (h) 2-2

It's Villa's Goal of the Season as Stiliyan Petrov drives the ball forward to the edge of the penalty and John sticks out his right foot to send a sensational side-foot volley flying over goalkeeper Steve Simonsen and into the roof of the net. No wonder he rates it among the best five goals of his career. It puts Villa two-up, as well, only for Stoke to hit back with two late goals.

11 TOTTENHAM HOTSPUR (h) 1-2

Another disappointing result but another excellent Carew goal as James Milner moves on to Stiliyan Petrov's 84th minute pass to deliver a centre which John heads in off the underside of the bar.

12 MANCHESTER UNITED (a) 2-3

John stuns Old Trafford into near silence – apart from the small contingent of Villa fans, that is – with a neat header into the bottom corner of the net after Gareth Barry controls Luke Young's pass superbly before turning away from two United players to provide a fine cross.

13 EVERTON (h) 3-3

An opportunist goal, John smashing the ball home from five yards after both Gareth Barry and Gabby Agbonlahor are unable to make proper contact with James Milner's hard low 32nd minute centre.

14 HULL CITY (h) 1-0

John is a match-winner against the struggling Tigers with a superbly executed goal on the counter attack. Gareth Barry starts the move from deep inside Villa's half with a pass to Ashley Young and the winger provides a centre which John diverts past former Villa keeper Boaz Myhill with a deft touch.

15 MIDDLESBROUGH (a) 1-1

John proves he can pounce in the tightest of situations, turning smartly to send a right-foot angled shot through a crowd of players after Stiliyan Petrov's teasing chip is clawed away by goalkeeper Brad Jones at The Riverside.

TALKING GREAT GOALS!

It's a great feeling to score for Villa, but can you identify these scorers from the things they said afterwards?

1 "My goal against Arsenal was the first time I'd scored with my left foot. I scored a handful of goals for Fulham but they were either with my right foot or my head."

2 "My goal at Wigan is up there with my best, although I've scored better, like my second against Villa a couple of seasons ago. I got both goals that day."

3 "I've taken a few penalties for England under-21s but I can't recall taking one at club level before the one at Gillingham."

4 "I'm not a selfish person. It's nice to get a goal occasionally but this game is all about winning. That's all that matters and it's all I want to do."

5 "I'd never scored more than one goal in a game before. I thought maybe I would score two at some point but to get three together was brilliant."

6 "I've scored five like that and one good one. My good one was for Middlesbrough against Tottenham."

7 "To score on my debut in front of nearly 30,000 fans gave me a great buzz. I'd had a bit of a goal drought for the reserves before the Zilina game, so I've been putting in extra work on the training pitch."

8 "When you join a new club you want to score goals and make the fans happy, particularly at home. Unfortunately, it's taken me nearly three years!"

9 "I've never scored on a debut before. I got one on my home debut for Wigan, but this one was really special."

10 "When Gabby played the ball to me, I could have run it into the corner to make sure we got a point. But we didn't want to settle for that. I've never been involved in a more dramatic game."

Answers on page 60

Claret and Blue Aces

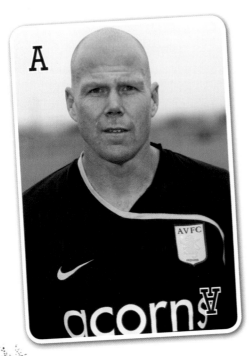

BRAD FRIEDEL

Born: LAKEWOOD, USA, 18/05/71

Position: GOALKEEPER

Signed for Villa: JULY 2008

Debut: HAFNARFJORDUR (a) UEFA Cup, 14/08/08

Previous clubs: GALATASARAY, COLUMBUS CREW, LIVERPOOL, BLACKBURN ROVERS

2008-09 record:
Appearances – 38 league, 8 cup

BRAD GUZAN

Born: CHICAGO, USA, 09/09/84
Position: GOALKEEPER
Signed for Villa: AUGUST 2008
Debut: QPR (h) Carling Cup 24/09/08
Previous clubs: CHIVAS USA

2008-09 record:
Appearances – 0 (1 sub) league, 7 cup

LUKE YOUNG

Born: HARLOW, 19/07/79
Position: FULL-BACK
Signed for Villa: AUGUST 2008
Debut: MANCHESTER CITY (h) 17/08/08
Previous clubs: TOTTENHAM HOTSPUR, CHARLTON ATHLETIC, MIDDLESBROUGH

2008-09 record:
Appearances – 33 (1 sub) league, 9 cup
Goals – 1 league

CARLOS CUELLAR

Born: MADRID, SPAIN, 23/08/81
Position: CENTRAL DEFENDER
Signed for Villa: AUGUST 2008
Debut: LITEX LOVECH (a) UEFA Cup, 18/09/08
Previous clubs: NURMANCIA, OSASUNA, GLASGOW RANGERS

2008-09 record:
Appearances – 24 (4 sub) league, 9 cup

CURTIS DAVIES

Born: LONDON, 15/03/85
Position: CENTRAL DEFENDER
Signed for Villa: AUGUST 2007
Debut: LEICESTER CITY (h)
League Cup 26/09/07
Previous clubs: LUTON TOWN,
WEST BROMWICH ALBION

2008-09 record:
Appearances – 34 (1 sub) league,
9 (1 sub) cup
Goals – 1 league

STEWART DOWNING

Born: MIDDLESBROUGH,
22/07/84
Position: WINGER
Signed for Villa: JULY 2009
Previous club:
MIDDLESBROUGH

WILFRED BOUMA

Born: HELMOND,
NETHERLANDS, 15/06/78
Position: FULL-BACK
Signed for Villa: AUGUST 2005
Debut: WEST HAM (a) 12/09/05
Previous club: PSV EINDHOVEN

2008-09 record:
Appearances – 2 cup

NICKY SHOREY

Born: ROMFORD, 19/02/81
Position: FULL-BACK
Signed for Villa: AUGUST 2008
Debut: HAFNARFJORDUR (a)
UEFA Cup, 14/08/08
Previous clubs: LEYTON
ORIENT, READING

2008-09 record:
Appearances – 19 (2 sub) league,
12 cup

STILIYAN PETROV

Born: BULGARIA, 05/07/79
Position: MIDFIELDER
Signed for Villa: AUGUST 2006
Debut: WEST HAM (a) 10/09/06
Previous clubs: CSKA SOFIA,
CELTIC

2008-09 record
Appearances – 36 league, 11 cup
Goals – 1 league, 1 cup

STEVE SIDWELL

Born: LONDON, 14/12/82
Position: MIDFIELDER
Signed for Villa: JULY 2008
Debut: ODENSE (a) Intertoto Cup,
19/07/08
Previous clubs: ARSENAL,
READING, CHELSEA

2008-09 record:
Appearances – 11 (5 sub) league,
9 cup
Goals – 3 league, 1 cup

JAMES MILNER

Born: LEEDS, 04/01/86
Position: MIDFIELDER
Signed for Villa: AUGUST 2008
Debut: LIVERPOOL (h), 31/08/08
Previous clubs: LEEDS UNITED,
NEWCASTLE UNITED

2008-09 record:
Appearances – 31 (5 sub) league,
6 (1 sub) cup
Goals – 3 league, 3 cup

CRAIG GARDNER

Born: BIRMINGHAM, 25/11/86
Position: MIDFIELDER
Signed pro: JANUARY 2005
Debut: EVERTON (h) 26/12/05,
Premiership
Previous clubs: None

2008-09 record:
Appearances – 3 (11 sub) league,
14 (2 sub) cup
Goals - 1 cup

NIGEL REO-COKER

Born: CROYDON, 14/05/84
Position: MIDFIELDER
Signed for Villa: JULY 2007
Debut: LIVERPOOL (h), 11/08/07
Previous clubs: WIMBLEDON,
WEST HAM UNITED

2008-09 record:
Appearances – 19 (7 sub) league,
10 cup
Goals - 1 league, 1 cup

ASHLEY YOUNG

Born: STEVENAGE, 09/07/85
Position: WINGER
Signed for Villa: JANUARY 2007
Debut: NEWCASTLE (a) 31/01/07
Previous club: WATFORD

2008-09 record:
Appearances – 36 league, 12 cup
Goals – 7 league, 2 cup

JOHN CAREW

Born: NORWAY, 05/09/79
Position: STRIKER
Signed for Villa: JANUARY 2007
Debut: NEWCASTLE (a) 31/01/07
Previous clubs: VALERNGEN, ROSENBORG, TRONDHEIM, VALENCIA, AS ROMA (loan), BESIKTAS, LYON.

2008-09 record:
Appearances – 18 (9 sub) league, 7 cup
Goals – 11 league, 4 cup

GABRIEL AGBONLAHOR

Born: BIRMINGHAM, 13/10/86
Position: STRIKER
Signed pro: FEBRUARY 2005
Debut: EVERTON (a) 18/03/05
Previous clubs: None

2008-09 record:
Appearances – 35 (1 sub) league, 10 (2 sub) cup
Goals – 12 league, 1 cup

EMILE HESKEY

Born: LEICESTER, 11/01/78
Position: STRIKER
Signed for Villa: JANUARY 2009
Debut: PORTSMOUTH (a) 27/01/09
Previous clubs: LEICESTER CITY, LIVERPOOL, BIRMINGHAM CITY, WIGAN ATHLETIC

2008-09 record:
Appearances – 11 (3 sub) league
Goals – 2 league

NATHAN DELFOUNESO

Born: BIRMINGHAM 02/02/91
Position: STRIKER
Signed professional: FEBRUARY 2008
Debut: HAFNARFJORDUR (a) 14/08/08, UEFA Cup
Previous clubs: NONE

2008-09 record:
Appearances – 0 (4 sub) league, 5 (4 sub) cup
Goals – 3 cup

MARLON HAREWOOD

Born: LONDON, 25/08/79
Position: STRIKER
Signed for Villa: JULY 2007
Debut: FULHAM (h) 25/08/07, Premier League
Previous clubs: NOTTINGHAM FOREST, WEST HAM UNITED

2008-09 record:
Appearances – 0 (6 sub) league, 6 (3 sub) cup
Goals – 1 cup

MOUSTAPHA SALIFOU

Born: LOME, TOGO, 01/06/83
Position: MIDFIELDER
Signed for Villa: AUGUST 2007
Debut: READING (h) 12/01/08
Premier League
Previous clubs: MODELE DE
LOME, RW OBERHAUSEN, STADE
BREST, WIL 1900

2008-09 record:
Appearances – 7 (2 sub) cup

ISAIAH OSBOURNE

Born: BIRMINGHAM, 05/11/87
Position: MIDFIELDER
Signed pro: NOVEMBER 2005
Debut: FULHAM (h) 21/10/06
Premiership
Previous clubs: NONE

2008-09 record:
Appearances – 3 (3 sub) cup

THE NAME GAME

CAN YOU UNRAVEL THESE ANAGRAMS TO
REVEAL THE NAMES OF VILLA PLAYERS?

1.   DRAB IF ELDER   **** *******

2.   CULL SOLAR RACE   ****** *******

3.   YIKES, ME HEEL!   ***** ******

4.   LOUNGE? YUK!   **** *****

5.   NANNY BAR BAR   ***** ******

6.   HEN FOUND A SLATE? NO   ****** **********

7.   VEST WILL SEED   ***** *******

8.   LINES JAMMER   ***** ******

9.   A RAMBLING TORCH   **** **********

10.   DUB GRAN A-Z   **** *****

The answers are on pages 60, but see if you can work them out without looking!

JOHN CAREW

ASHLEY'S AWARDS

A few eyebrows were raised when Villa signed Ashley Young from Watford for an initial £8m, rising to £9.6m based on appearances and international caps. But he has proved to be worth every penny.

After a fairly low-key start to life in claret and blue, the flying winger really came good when he was given a roving role behind the strikers during his first full season for the club.

And he got even better last season, producing some sizzling performances which brought him nine goals, a host of "assists" – and a trio of awards.

He was voted Barclays Player of the Month in both September and December, and in April he landed an even more prestigious prize when he was named the PFA Young Footballer of the Year.

Needless to say, he was absolutely delighted with all three trophies. Particularly as the PFA award came as something of a surprise to him, even when he and his pal Gabby Agbonlahor were both among the players on the short list.

"I didn't think I was going to win it," he said. "It was a great honour to win such a massive award.

"It was great to receive the Player of the Month awards, as well. It really helps your confidence when you get things like that. But football is a team game and without all the lads around me I wouldn't have done it."

Ashley, in fact, collected THREE Player of the Month awards during 2008, also getting the vote for April, and that's something which had never been achieved before.

Ashley actually started his Villa career as a striker, scoring on his debut at Newcastle in January 2007, although he has no real preference over positions.

"As long as I'm in the starting line-up, I'm happy," he says. "It doesn't really matter whether I'm on the right, the left, behind the front two or up front. It doesn't matter as long as I'm doing well for the team."

ASHLEY YOUNG

NICE ONE, NATHAN!

He's still only 18 but Nathan Delfouneso looks set for a glittering career in claret and blue after being voted the club's Young Player of the Year for 2008-09. The Birmingham-born striker marked his breakthrough to Villa's first team with a superb goal – a stunning left-foot volley – on his full debut and has continued to impress. He tells us about his career so far.

Who was your hero as a boy?

Even though I supported Manchester United, Thierry Henry was my favourite player. I really enjoyed watching him and I tried to model my own game on him. When I was given a squad number by Villa and I was told 14 was available, that was the one for me because it's what Henry wears. You can imagine how thrilled I was last season when a French magazine compared me with him – it showed I must be doing something right!

How old were you when you joined Villa's Academy?

I was eight. I'm not sure who spotted me, but one day my dad asked if I would like to start training with Villa. I had a successful trial so I started training once or twice a week. We also had a game at the weekend.

Have you always been a striker?

At times I've played in midfield but yes, predominantly I've always been a striker. I've scored my fair share of goals for Villa's Academy and reserve teams and hopefully I can get a lot more for the first team.

What honours have you won so far?

The reserves have won the league for the past two years and last season we became national champions by beating Sunderland 3-1 in the play-off final. I was delighted to score one of the goals. Before that, I was in the youth side who won the Hong Kong Sevens and a tournament in Germany.

Tell us about your first team debut.

I went on as a substitute in a couple of early season games, but my full debut was against MSK Zilina in the UEFA Cup. It turned out brilliantly for me because I scored our goal in a 1-1 draw. It was a great feeling to score on my debut in front of a big crowd. My dad and my younger brother Emmitt were at the game, which made it even more special. I must admit I was a bit surprised to be in the line-up because I hadn't started a first team game before, but it was a very proud night for me.

What's your biggest ambition?

I really want to become a regular member of the Villa team and keep improving my game. It would be nice if we could win a trophy, as well!

What does it mean to you to be a Villa player?

It means a lot because I've been here since I was eight and I've come through the system. The Villa Academy coaches do a great job, as you can see from the players who have come through over the past few years.

What advice would you give to any youngster wanting to be a professional footballer?

The most important things are hard work and dedication. You have to make sure you do all the right things, technically, fitness-wise and mentally. Just before my debut, for instance, I'd had a bit of a goal drought in the reserves so I put in some extra work on the training pitch. Sometimes I used to hit balls at an empty net, just to make sure I was striking them properly. It didn't really matter that there wasn't a goalkeeper – and it paid off when I scored against Zilina.

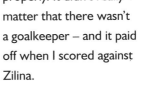

QUIZ TIME!

How closely were you watching your heroes last season? Here's a quiz to test what you can remember about Villa's 2008-09 campaign. Most of the answers can be found on other pages in this annual – but see how many you can get right without any help!

1. Which player scored a hat-trick in the opening Premier League match of the season against Manchester City at Villa Park?

2. Who scored Villa's fastest goal of the season?

3. Who were the club's Player of the Season and Young Player of the Season?

4. Six Villa players were named in Fabio Capello's England squad for a friendly against Spain in February. Can you name them?

5. From which club did Luke Young join Villa?

6. Villa created a club record number of away league wins when they beat Blackburn Rovers 2-0 at Ewood Park. Can you remember the number of victories in their record-breaking sequence?

7. Which Villa player was voted the PFA Young Player of the Season?

8. Villa reached the last 32 of the UEFA Cup before losing to CSKA Moscow. But which Danish club did they beat in the Intertoto Cup, right at the start of their European adventure?

9. A player who scored in the Intertoto tie was forced to retire at the end of the season because of injury. His name?

10. What was Villa's position in the final table – fifth, sixth or seventh?

Answers on pages 60

STEVE SIDWELL

45

WHAT A START!

Steve and Emile join the Premier Debut Club

Any footballer will tell you that scoring on your debut is an incredible feeling – and it's certainly not something which happens on a regular basis. That's why Steve Sidwell and Emile Heskey had reason to celebrate last season.

The 2008-09 campaign was the 17th season of Premier League football, and during all that time only 15 Villa players had hit the target in their first league game for the club – an average of less than one a year.

But Steve and Emile both achieved the feat in the space of the same season. Steve was on target after going on as a substitute in the 4-0 victory at Wigan Athletic in October, while Emile hit the only goal in Villa's 1-0 win at Portsmouth in January.

Although he had signed from Chelsea during the summer, Steve had to wait for his first Premier action in a Villa shirt, having been sidelined by injury after playing the Intertoto Cup games against Danish club Odense in July.

But England international Emile lined up at Fratton Park just a few days after arriving from Wigan – and his stunning 20-yard shot ensured that Villa headed back from the south coast with all three points.

"It was a great start for me," said the former Leicester City and Liverpool player. "I'd never scored on my debut before. I got one on my home debut for Wigan against Reading, but this one was really special. I was really excited when I scored."

IT'S A FACT

• Strictly speaking, Dalian Atkinson scored on his Premier League debut, hitting the equaliser at Ipswich in the club's first game in the new league in 1992. But he had already played for Villa in the old First Division the previous season.

• Dion Dublin made it a double on his debut, scoring twice against Tottenham. He went on to score seven goals in his first three games – a club record.

PREMIER DEBUT SCORERS

Player	Debut	Date	Result
JOHN FASHANU	Everton (a)	20/08/94	**2-2**
MARK DRAPER	Man Utd (h)	19/08/95	**3-1**
PAUL MERSON	Wimbledon (h)	12/09/98	**2-0**
DION DUBLIN (2)	Tottenham (h)	07/11/98	**3-2**
LUC NILIS	Chelsea (h)	27/08/00	**1-1**
STEFAN MOORE	Charlton (h)	11/09/02	**2-0**
JOEY GUDJONSSON	Middlesbrough(a)	28/01/03	**5-2**
CARLTON COLE	Southampton (h)	14/08/04	**2-0**
KEVIN PHILLIPS	Bolton (h)	13/08/05	**2-2**
MILAN BAROS	Blackburn (h)	27/08/05	**1-0**
GABBY AGBONLAHOR	Everton (a)	18/03/06	**1-4**
ASHLEY YOUNG	Newcastle (a)	31/01/07	**1-3**
ZAT KNIGHT	Chelsea (h)	02/09/07	**2-0**
STEVE SIDWELL	Wigan (a)	26/10/08	**4-0**
EMILE HESKEY	Portsmouth (a)	27/01/09	**1-0**

EMILE HESKEY

WELL HOW ABOUT THAT!

FASCINATING FACTS FROM LAST SEASON

GABBY'S QUICKFIRE HAT-TRICK

Sharp-shooter Gabby Agbonlahor wrote himself into the record books with a quickfire hat-trick in a 4-2 home win over Manchester City in Villa's first Premier League match of the season.

Gabby scored in the 68th, 74th and 76th minutes, which made it the second fastest hat-trick since the Premier League started in 1992. Only Robbie Fowler, for Liverpool against Arsenal in 1994, had scored a Premier League hat-trick in a shorter space of time. More significantly, from a Villa point of view, it was the first time for 78 years that anyone had scored three times on the opening day of the season. The previous player to achieve the feat was Tom "Pongo" Waring, who scored all four in a 4-3 victory over Manchester United on the opening day of the 1930-31 campaign.

STEVE'S SO SHARP

Steve Sidwell was on target after just 31 seconds of Villa's 3-2 victory over Everton at Goodison Park, which made him the Premier League's fastest scorer of the season. Ashley Young hit the winner in the final minute of stoppage time – and it was the first time Villa had ever won a match by taking a first-minute lead and grabbing a last-minute winner.

LONG-RUNNING BRAD

Goalkeeper Brad Friedel created Premier League history when he made his 167th consecutive league appearance in Villa's home match against Fulham, breaking a record previously held by former Villa goalkeeper David James. Most of the games in Brad's record-breaking sequence were for his previous club Blackburn Rovers, but we were delighted that he achieved his milestone while playing for Villa!

MARTIN'S THE TOP DANE

Martin Laursen, who sadly had to retire at the end of the season because of a knee injury, won two Danish Footballer of the Year awards. And while he was delighted with both, he was particularly pleased with the second because the votes were cast by other Danish players.

A WORK OF ART

Maybe you've painted some big pictures at school, but surely nothing like this? A huge painting of Villa Park, measuring 9m high by 4m wide, was unveiled in the Trinity Road stand reception area in September.

It was painted by renowned artist Stephen Farthing, who based his work on the famous Lowry painting "Going to the Match".

Even Stephen didn't know how the complete picture would look until it was displayed on the wall in the Trinity Road stand reception area. He painted it in eight separate sections – and had to climb scaffolding to put the finishing touches!

AWAY THE LADS!

Villa established a club record seven consecutive league away wins when they won 2-0 against Blackburn Rovers in February with goals from James Milner and Gabby Agbonlahor. A special first day postal cover was produced to mark the achievement. The team's other wins in the "lucky seven" record-breaking sequence were at Arsenal (2-0), Everton (3-2), West Ham (1-0), Hull City (1-0), Sunderland (2-1) and Portsmouth (1-0).

SIX OF THE BEST

Six Villa players – Gareth Barry, Emile Heskey, Ashley Young, James Milner, Gabby Agbonlahor and Luke Young – were called up by Fabio Capello for the original squad for England's friendly against Spain in February. Never before had so many Villans figured in an England squad, although only Barry and Heskey played in Seville.

BEST FOR 13 YEARS

Villa's points total of 62 was the club's highest since 1995-96, when they finished fourth with 63. The highest during the Premier League years was 74 in 1992-93, when they were runners-up to Manchester United.

STAN'S THE MAN

FANS' FAVOURITE – STILIYAN PROUDLY CLUTCHES THE NEW TERRACE TROPHY

No doubt you have heard the old saying: "If at first you don't succeed, try, try again."

We're not sure if there's a similar phrase in Bulgaria but Stiliyan Petrov seems to know all about it. Villa's talented midfielder spent the best part of two seasons striving to reproduce the form which persuaded manager Martin O'Neill to sign him from Celtic – largely without success.

Stiliyan - known to his team-mates as Stan – enjoyed a fantastic debut against West Ham at Upton Park but then, hard as he tried, he struggled to find his best form.

But all that changed last season. With his confidence boosted by a magnificent 45-yard goal at Derby towards the end of the 2007-08 campaign, he began to conjure up the dominant displays which had made him such an important figure for his previous clubs and his country.

Stiliyan was one of the main reasons Villa challenged for a top four Premier League place for most of the season and enjoyed an extended run in the UEFA Cup.

His contribution didn't go unnoticed – either by his playing colleagues or by Villa fans. At the club's annual awards night, he was presented with both the Players' Player of the Year and Supporters' Player of the Year trophies.

And a couple of weeks later he made it a hat-trick when he became the first player to receive the Terrace Trophy, an award which has been revived by the Lions Clubs, complete with a brand new trophy.

"It was a big thing for me to win those awards, especially after the way my career started at Villa," says Stiliyan. "People expected more and I didn't produce it, which was frustrating.

"But I came here as a good player and that was how I wanted people to regard me. I never stopped believing."

The last player to receive the old trophy was Dennis Mortimer back in 1977, and Mortimer went on to lead Villa to both the League Championship in 1981 and the European Cup in 1982.

So Stiliyan is in good company, and he would certainly have no complaints and he certainly has time to do it, having signed a new four-year contract just before the end of last season.

He was also delighted to score his first goal at Villa Park in March – his first on home soil since he arrived from Celtic in August 2006. And although it wasn't quite as sensational as his long-range goal at Derby, his sizzling shot against Stoke City was still pretty special – particularly after it had taken him so long.

"That was a great feeling," he says. "When you join a new club you want to score goals and make the fans happy. Unfortunately it took me nearly three years!

"It obviously wasn't as spectacular as my goal at Derby but the feeling was just the same. I'm a bit surprised I haven't scored more for Villa. I scored 63 for Celtic and it would be great to get more here.

"This is the best league in the world and I'm really enjoying playing in it."

STILIYAN PETROV

VILLANS IN THE FRAME

The Stick Man

A goalkeeper is often referred to as "the man between the sticks". So Brad Friedel could hardly have made a more appropriate choice when he was asked to select a book as Villa's Premier League Reading Stars ambassador.

The book the American keeper chose as his children's selection was called "The Stick Man" – although he assures us the link with his position is purely coincidental. It just happens that his daughter enjoyed having the book read to her!

Mia's a natural

Stan Collymore was Villa's record signing when he arrived from Liverpool for £7m in 1997. These days he does his talking off the pitch – as a presenter for Talk Sport Radio – and it looks like his seven-year-old daughter Mia could also have a future in broadcasting.

Stan brought Mia along to her first Villa match towards the end of last season, and in between his commentary on the match and his chat show, he popped a pair of headphones on her and gave her his microphone. It looks like she's a natural!

Villa's cup winners

Most of us can only imagine what it would be like to win a trophy for Villa but these youngsters have actually done it!

They represented the club at the Premier League Schools Tournament finals – and beat Bolton Wanderers 1-0 in the final of the under-11 mixed section.

Each of the 20 Premier League clubs staged their own competition to select a school to represent them in the regional finals, and in Villa's case it was Dorridge Junior School.

From there, eight teams in each section made it through to the national finals at Old Trafford. They got ready in the dressing rooms used by Manchester United before walking down the tunnel into the Theatre of Dreams.

And as the winning teams received their trophies, Queen's famous anthem "We are the Champions" blasted out over the PA system.

Jordan spots Fabio

Fabio Capello has regularly watched Villa since becoming England manager and at one stage last season he called up no fewer than six players from Martin O'Neill's squad.

Fabio's search for international talent meant he was a frequent visitor to Villa Park – and on one occasion it was the England boss who got "spotted".

When Villa fan Jordan Goodridge saw him, she couldn't resist asking for a photo!

A perfect pitch…

The Villa Park playing surface is Jonathan Calderwood's pride and joy – because he's the man responsible for keeping it in tip-top condition.

The club's grounds manager has certainly done that over the past few years, and last season it only narrowly missed out on being voted Premier League Pitch of the Year.

The top prize went to Arsenal but the efforts of Jonathan and his staff ensured that Villa Park was the runner-up.

Made in England...

Villa have provided more England players than any other club, and that impressive fact was the inspiration behind the design for this season's away kit.

By the end of last season, 67 Villa players had proudly represented their country. It all began way back in 1888, when Howard Vaughton hit five goals and Arthur Brown netted four in a 13-0 demolition of Ireland.

More recently, the likes of Emile Heskey, Ashley Young and Gabby Agbonlahor have all played for the national side, so Nike's design team based the new away kit on England's colours.

Villa players were actually forced to change into their third choice white kit for one match last season – even though they were at home.

The unusual situation arose when referee Rob Styles refused to allow West Ham to wear their all-blue kit because the sleeves clashed with the blue on Villa's sleeves.

The Hammers didn't have any other kit with them, so a set of white shirts – which the players had previously worn only in their UEFA Cup-tie in Moscow – had to be quickly prepared for Martin O'Neill's men.

Villa actually kicked off in shirts which did not have their names on the back or the Premier League logo on the sleeves. But members of the club's merchandising staff spent the first half preparing another set, which the players wore after the half-time break.

Villa also wore their regular white shorts, which meant they were in all-white for a home match for the first time since the UEFA Cup-tie against Atletico Madrid 11 years earlier.

FIND THE EUROSTARS!

Villa had 12 heroes when they won the European Cup in 1982. Can you find the players who secured a 1-0 victory over Bayern Munich on that memorable night in Rotterdam? The names you should find in this word search are:

**RIMMER • SPINK • SWAIN • EVANS • McNAUGHT
MORTIMER • WILLIAMS • BREMNER • COWANS
MORLEY • WITHE • SHAW**

```
M  W  I  L  L  I  A  M  S  A
C  O  M  O  R  L  E  Y  P  Q
N  B  R  Z  T  S  W  A  I  N
A  R  I  T  C  O  W  A  N  S
U  E  M  K  I  P  D  N  K  H
G  M  M  G  E  M  H  L  J  A
H  N  E  A  V  M  E  A  Q  W
T  E  R  S  A  T  U  R  L  V
Z  R  D  E  N  F  W  O  R  G
B  A  T  N  S  W  I  T  H  E
```

Can you work out who's had their faces warped?

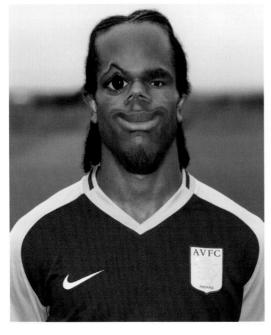

Answers on pages 60 and 61

SPOT THE DIFFERENCE

Can you find the seven differences between these two images?

Answers on page 60

SECOND TO NONE!

We sometimes call Villa's reserves the second string – but they are most certainly not second best.

Under the guidance of coach Kevin MacDonald, the claret and blue youngsters have swept all before them over the past couple of years.

They have won the FA Premier Reserve League South title two years running and last season they went a step further, being crowned national champions after beating North section champions Sunderland 3-1 in the final.

It was a fabulous night, more than 5,000 people turning up at Villa Park to see Villa beat the Black Cats with goals from Nathan Delfouneso, James Collins and Shane Lowry.

It also made up for the disappointment of 12 months earlier, when Villa finished top of the table but lost to Liverpool at Anfield in the final.

If victory in the 2009 final was the highlight of a wonderful campaign, though, MacDonald stressed that it wasn't merely a one-off.

"I'm ecstatic about the lads' hard work throughout the year," he said, as his players celebrated their magnificent achievement. "They enjoy working with each other and they enjoy each other's success. That's a big thing.

"They have to enjoy these things, savour it and say 'I want more of that'."

The side remained consistent throughout the season, losing just two league matches and it was very much a team effort, with no single player grabbing all the glory. The team netted 29 goals in their league games – and those goals were shared between 15 different scorers!

CARLOS CUELLAR

CHEESY KEEPER!

Here's a recipe for a tasty savoury treat which should keep young Villa fans occupied on a rainy day...

WHAT YOU WILL NEED

100g (4 oz) self raising flour
75g (3 oz) hard cheese (grated)
50g (2 oz) butter or margarine
1 beaten egg
Pinch of salt
Dab of mustard
Thinly chopped lettuce to serve

WHAT TO DO

(1) Mix flour, salt and mustard together, then rub in the margarine or butter.

(2) Mix in most of the cheese, and add enough egg to make a stiff dough.

(3) Roll out very thinly and cut half of the pastry into long strips.

(4) Put the strips together to make a goal shape.

(5) Cut out a body shape, with big gloves, and also a ball shape. Take the odd bits of pastry, roll it into a very thin sausage shape. Then use it to make some hair and to write AV on the shirt.

(6) Place on a greased tray, put your keeper into the shape you want, sprinkle the rest of the cheese on top, and bake for 10-15 minutes at 180°C, 350°F or Gas Mark 4 until golden brown.

(7) Allow to cool, then lay your goalie on the plate of chopped lettuce, ready to make a save!

Bet you eat this before half-time!

Lion's Score!

Hercules just made an awesome run and scored a belter! Which path did he take to score the goal?

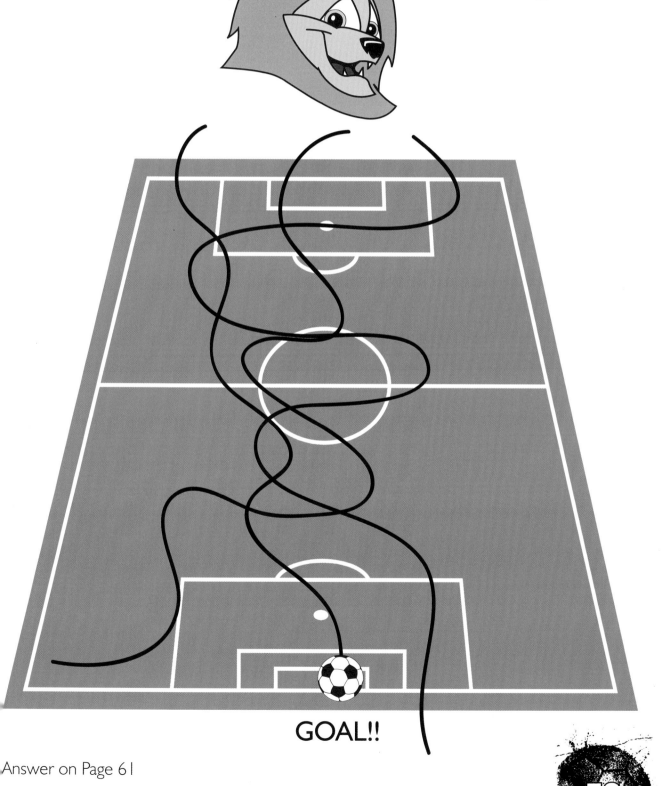

GOAL!!

Answer on Page 61

How did you get on?

Spot the Difference P55

Warped Faces P54

Nathan Delfouneso and Gabby Agbonlahor

Word Search P54

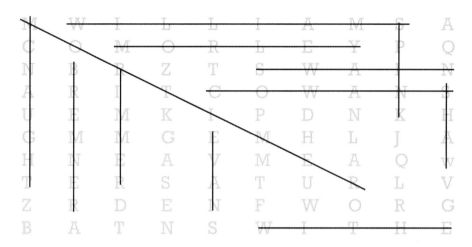

Page 59
Who scored?

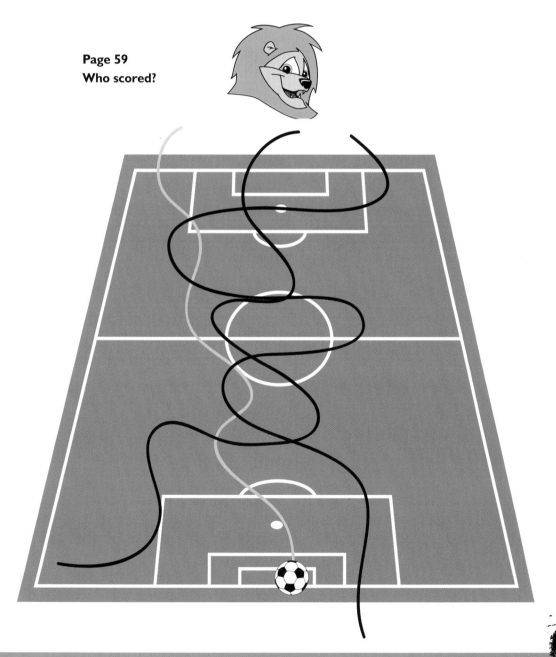